anthology
of concretism

anthology
of concretism

EDITED BY EUGENE WILDMAN

Introduction by PETER MICHELSON

Afterword by EUGENE WILDMAN

Second Revised and Enlarged Edition

THE SWALLOW PRESS, INC.

CHICAGO

This anthology is a revised and enlarged version of
the volume 19, number 4 issue of the *Chicago Re-
view*. Swallow Press' first revised and enlarged edi-
tion, entitled THE CHICAGO REVIEW ANTHOLOGY OF
CONCRETISM, contained additional contributors, an
Afterword, and some slight rearrangements. Swal-
low Press' second revised and enlarged edition, en-
titled ANTHOLOGY OF CONCRETISM, adds an Intro-
duction and more pieces by contributors.

Printed in the United States of America.

ACKNOWLEDGMENTS

Grateful acknowledgment is made to the *Chicago
Review* and to the Division of Humanities of The
University of Chicago for their very generous per-
mission and cooperation in the publication of this
volume.

Special thanks are due to Alain Arias-Misson, who
was the main link with the poets and who permitted
himself to be used as a kind of international postal
clearing house when the original *Chicago Review*
issue was being compiled. Leonard Shaykin, who
was traveling in Europe at the time, helped initiate
the original correspondence.

The calligraphy accompanying the poems of Seiichi
Niikuni and Kitasono Katué is by Hiroaki Morino,
formerly the ceramicist at The University of
Chicago's Midway Studios.

contents

introduction

Crowding establishment perimeters as it does, the posture of an experimental poetry is, willy-nilly, nearly always aggressive. Perhaps, therefore, an introduction to a book of experimental poems should try to reduce this natural abrasion, hoping to get so exploratory an art and its audience past at least *that* fruitless idol. Because this is in effect *The Chicago Review Anthology of Concretism*'s third edition in the last two years, such a task has been in part already done. Still, concretism has its enemies. Erich Kahler finds in it the prime illustrations of what he calls "the triumph of incoherence," in his recent book *The Disintegration of Form in the Arts*. Mr. Kahler's able and probably representative attack on contemporary poetics reminds us that much new artistic theory and practice *is* exploratory and perhaps therefore even as yet incomplete. So it is likely to find a largely skeptical or hostile audience. That it may be construed to threaten traditional values is easy enough to understand, but that it *need not* should also be understood. What is true from our tradition will always survive. But there is no reason to suppose either that we do now know or that at any time we have known our tradition and its implications fully. Nor need we suppose that the tradition itself demands a single, univocal artistic theory. Even Aristotle, the very heart of traditional western poetics, acknowledged that poetic form was evolutionary when he said that he did not know if poetry had "as yet perfected its proper types." This problem—of dynamic form—has been one of the grand motifs in the history of literary criticism. Dryden's resolution of that long time issue provides intelligent principles of procedure for all ages. In preferring "moderns" to "ancients" he refers us to not only the refinements of craft that history has brought, but also to the cultural development of taste that will determine the nature of the artistic audience, without which there is no art. That much artistic sophistication even the law courts allow when they refer judgments of pornography to "contemporary community standards." And what good, after all, is a poetic tradition that doesn't give us improvement with time, that *future* test of past and present to which tradition unfailingly refers us.

The business of an experimental poetics is to explore radical changes and possibilities in both its vision and its manner. If we find, as many have, that our vision has lost confidence in a coherent and esthetically pleasing moral scheme, then we should not be surprised to find, as many have, that the old mimetic modes have forfeited their ultimate authority. For many poets and critics the absence of convincing poetic or moral authority is itself a call for exploratory poetics. If such exploration looses our demi-urge, as Kahler suggests, then we must candidly know that Dionysius lives in us, as we have been forewarned by poets, prophets, and psychologists. And now that his weapon has nuclear power we needs must see him face to face. So we find a way. Kahler, fearing "anarchy" and "chaos," tells us: "We are confronted with an ever increasing mass of unmastered life-material, without and within ourselves. What we must do today above all . . . is to gather all our resources for the mastery of our world, which means directing our efforts toward establishing rather than dissevering and dissecting coherences." The "master" metaphor, however, is fascistic and humanistically self defeating. But if ever we can under any circumstances, it is certain that we *cannot* "master" our life-material by ignoring Dionysian energy or its anarchical and chaotic analogues. Such terms as *anarchy* and *chaos* designate archetypal evils that have never existed in fact, and never will. They are proximate concepts. If, therefore, we sense these qualities in modern life, we must, if we are not to make bogeys of them, distinguish between their material and their mythic natures. The proper historical context, then, in which to see concretism is as one instance in the poetic search for meaning in material—the stuff marking the difference, after all, between keeping and giving up the ghost.

Concrete poetry, as its name implies, is a poetry of material. At its best, its most ambitious (as in Jean Francois Bory's "veux," pp. 131 ff.), it is a visual metaphor of modern sensibility—the "red shift," the center falling apart. It may also be "literary," as Bory's poem is, but it is even before that *material*. For example, though I have "read" Bory's poem perhaps ten times, I have not yet read all its "words." Its first physical appearance gives coherence to, provides a center for, and thus defines, the page. Soon, however, it takes over the page—dominating it with shape, shade, and even the tease of imagery, symbolism, and other "literary" paraphernalia. But no sooner is it "master" than it explodes, moving our consciousness beyond the edge of the book, ending one step short of its logical conclusion—the denial of not only the arbitrary authority of *page* but of all perceptive possibility. That "charitable" ending is the ultimate artistic statement, the artist controlling reality for his own purposes, intimidated neither by logic nor metaphysics, responsible rather to his own sense of reality than to rules of validity. Does such a poem—and we haven't even touched on its literary dimension—dissever coherences? Perhaps, but coherence, often called Beauty, is just where it has always been—in the eye of its beholder. The material presence of Bory's poem, like many concrete poems, alludes to and questions both the need for and humanistic *value* of "coherence."

For the other side of the "coherence" coin, after all, is system, bureaucracy, mechanization, and the whole modernistic programming apparatus by which personality is reduced to number and humanistic idiosyncracy is compressed into productive function. The concrete poet fights back. In declining to let printing efficiency rule his poem's physique or in declining to let spatial economy determine its physical density, he grapples with the possibility of true organic form, form not controlled by the systematic efficiency of the printing trade. In short, as the poet becomes his own printer (which literally is true in this book, where the poems are photographically reproduced from the poet's own "manuscript"), he is at one with not only its symbolic but also its material form. He has demechanized the material cause of his poetry. His Dionysian will has scattered the printer's type, shattered his plates, unlocked his page frames, and given the inevitable finger to economy. The poet has thus become united with his poem in a way that he has not been since the troubadors. So much so that the concretist asks his "reader" to stand on his head if necessary to read it. For now the poem is closer than ever to his pure imagination; and it may be responsible therefore to its essential self, not to such esthetic irrelevancies as gravity or overtime. If Industry's sensibilities—or those of the engineer—are dissociated, the poetic imagination has gone a long way toward putting body and soul together. Concretism, and the poetics of which it is a part, show us how we can come to humanistic terms with our technocratic ethos. When the bureaucrats have us up against the wall, as they always do, then simply deny their reality—write a round poem (pp. 131-43), or a design poem (pp. 71-3), or a pun poem (pp. 25 or 69), or a sound poem (p. 79).

Give Caesar what's his. But do not under any circumstances forfeit the fun of mix-mattering media. Do not forfeit the fun of finding the reality that made the computer that programmed the personality that told us to *produce* or go back where we came from. Don't, for any chimerical coherence, forfeit the fun that distinguishes *you* from the industrious role our ant-hill societies impose for their banal, destructive ends. When the order of the day is "Fall In," don't do it. Play games instead. Don't even make mudpies—that's just another kind of production line. Reality sandwiches, says the poet, can be eaten only by properly humane players. And if such playing seems evasive, remember what the poet has also told us—that feeling human in the midst of *things* is a useful form of political subversion. That's where concrete poetry is at—making *things* conform to the human imagination.

This book itself is an educative experience. It is more than a concretist anthology. It is, as the Afterword says, a concrete Book. That is the peculiar quality that distinguishes it from other concrete collections. The format, the book's plan and character, complement its substance. Thereby the editor's own education at the hands of his material is documented. All things being at rest, an editor puts poems into a book. The book, thus, *contains* the poems. Here, however, the book is itself a poem. As Eugene Wildman, then editor of the *Chicago Review*, gathered material for this anthology he responded to it in kind, and quickly recognized that this book could not merely be a container, but must be an environment integrating the poems with their physical location and that location with its audience. The editor learned the concretist's primer lesson: how to demechanize not only his editorial function but also the very machinery that produces his book.

I have already observed that this is the third edition of this anthology, which simply confirms that it is telling something to somebody. I know it talks persuasively to fellow teachers of literature. And I know it is saying important things to students. It says to those who suppose poetry had reached dead end: Look again. It says to those who thought poetry—either the tightly reined New Critical or the galloping Beat kind—was dull or pretentious or "hard": Have fun, play games, it will do you good. It says to those who have long been taught to lock their experience into categories: Loosen up, look around, poetry is an art that means to help you *live*, not an object certifying your own high brow. I have used this book as a text for courses in literary criticism.

Colleagues of mine have used it in modern poetry courses and in design and drawing courses. The results are uniform; concretism not only opens up students it also opens up teachers to new artistic perspectives. But, to put this testimonial on a properly high plane, let me indicate the instructive dividends of concretism by quoting a passage from an undergraduate paper:

> Now for a manifesto. From what I have seen and vicariously felt, I think most Concrete poets will agree: Now, friends, we are here to proclaim the word in space—in inner space and outer space. We proclaim the word as well as proclaiming the emptiness around it. When we say "line of poetry," we mean line as line and not as length of sound. And to "color a thought" is no longer a metaphor but real live color. If our words do not touch you, then you should touch them, feel them, even play with them. If our words do not move you, then you should move them. Poetry is not "in the air." It is not everywhere. Poetry, friends, is where it is at.

Finally, however, one should not read this book because it will teach him something. He should read it because it will be a pleasure. But, being pleased, if he should also be taught what pleases him and be encouraged by that pleasure to seek more gold in poetry's hills than he expected to find, well there is no harm in that.

Peter Michelson
April 1969

Peter Michelson attended Whitman College, the University of Wyoming, and The University of Chicago. He has been editor of the CHICAGO REVIEW, *has taught literature at Northwestern University and at Roosevelt University, and is at present on the faculty of the University of Notre Dame. He is author of numerous essays and of the book,* PORNOGRAPHY, AN ESSAY IN GENRE. *He is also represented in Swallow Press'* NEW POETRY ANTHOLOGY I.

rain

雨

川
州

stream
bank

川川川川川川川川川川川川川川川川川川川川川
川川川川川川川川川川川川川川川川川川川川州
川川川川川川川川川川川川川川川川川川州州
川川川川川川川川川川川川川川川川川州州州
川川川川川川川川川川川川川川川川州州州州
川川川川川川川川川川川川川川川州州州州州
川川川川川川川川川川川川川川州州州州州州
川川川川川川川川川川川川州州州州州州州州
川川川川川川川川川川川州州州州州州州州州
川川川川川川川川川川州州州州州州州州州州
川川川川川川川川川州州州州州州州州州州州
川川川川川川川川州州州州州州州州州州州州
川川川川川川川州州州州州州州州州州州州州
川川川川川川州州州州州州州州州州州州州州
川川川川川州州州州州州州州州州州州州州州
川川川川州州州州州州州州州州州州州州州州
川川川州州州州州州州州州州州州州州州州州
川川州州州州州州州州州州州州州州州州州州
川州州州州州州州州州州州州州州州州州州州
州州州州州州州州州州州州州州州州州州州州

ADRIANO SPATOLA

```
i i i i i i i i i ì
i i i i i i i i ì ì
i i i i i i i ì ì ì
i i i i i i ì ì ì ì
i i i i i ì ì ì ì ì
i i i i ì ì ì ì ì ì
i i i ì ì ì ì ì ì ì
i i ì ì ì ì ì ì ì ì
i ì ì ì ì ì ì ì ì ì
ì ì ì ì ì ì ì ì ì ì
i ì ì ì ì ì ì ì ì ì
i i ì ì ì ì ì ì ì ì
i i i ì ì ì ì ì ì ì
i i i i ì ì ì ì ì ì
i i i i i ì ì ì ì ì
i i i i i i ì ì ì ì
i i i i i i i ì ì ì
i i i i i i i i ì ì
i i i i i i i i i ì
```

```
é    è
é    è
é    è
é    è
é    è
é    è
é    è
é    è
é    è
   e e e
    e e
   e e e
    e e
     e
```

```
ôôôôôôôôôôôôôô
ôôôôôôôôôôôôô^o
ôôôôôôôôôôôô^^oo
ôôôôôôôôôôô^^^ooo
ôôôôôôôôôô^^^^oooo
ôôôôôôôôô^^^^^ooooo
ôôôôôôôô^^^^^^oooooo
ôôôôôôô^^^^^^^ooooooo
ôôôôôô^^^^^^^^oooooooo
ôôôôô^^^^^^^^^ooooooooo
ôôôô^^^^^^^^^^oooooooooo
ôôô^^^^^^^^^^^ooooooooooo
ôô^^^^^^^^^^^^oooooooooooo
ô^^^^^^^^^^^^^ooooooooooooo
^^^^^^^^^^^^^^oooooooooooooo
```

HANSJÖRG MAYER

arizqhypgxofwnevm dulctkbsj
gxofwnevmdulctkbs jarizqhyp
ndulctkbsjarizqhy pgxofwnev
bsjarizqhypgxofwn evmdulctk
hypgxofwnevmdulct kbsjarizq
nevmdulctkbsjariz qhypgxofw
ctkbsjarizqhypgxo fwnevmdul
zqhypgxofwnevmdu lctkbsjar
ofwnevmdulctkbsja rizqhypgx
dulctkbsjarizqhyp gxofwnevm
jarizqhypgxofwnev mdulctkbs
pgxofwnevmdulctkb sjarizqhy
evmdulctkbsjariza hypgxofwn
kbsjarizqhypgxofw nevmdulct
qhypgxofwnevmdulc tkbsjariz
fwnevmdulctkbsjar izqhypgxo
ctkbsjarizqhypgx ofwnevmdu

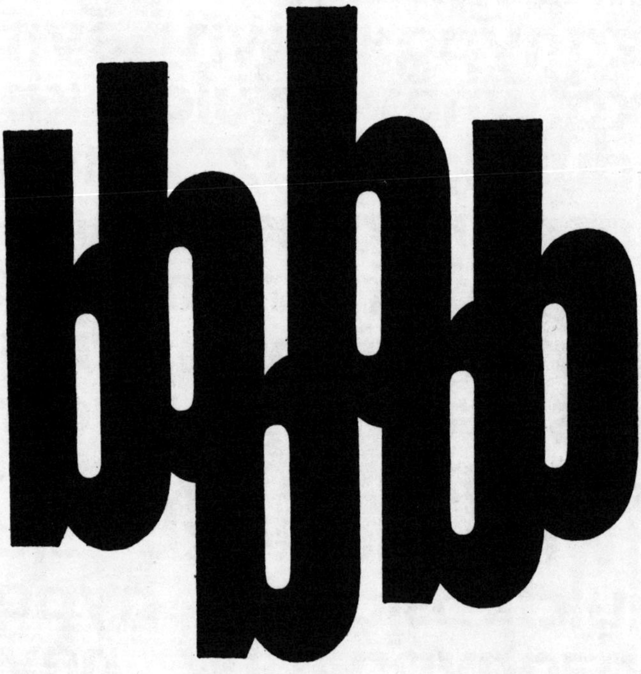

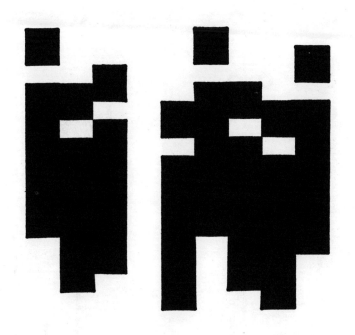

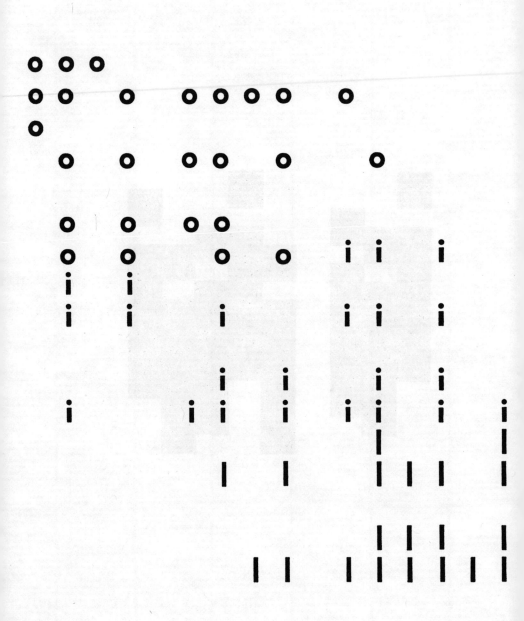

sau
aus
usa

Blod

wwww

wwww

....

waww

wakw

wake

....

walw

walk

lighght

```
crickets
crickess
cricksss
cricssss
crisssss
crsssss
csssssss
ssssssss
ssssssts
ssssssets
sssskets
sssckets
ssickets
srickets
crickets
```

crickets
crickets
crickets
crickets
crickets
crickets
crickets
crickets
crickets
crickets
crickets
crickets
crickets
crickets
crickets
crickets
crickets
crickets
crickets
crickets
crickets
crickets
crickets
crickets
crickets
crickets
crickets
crickets
crickets
crickets
crickets
crickets
crickets
crickets
crickets
crickets
crickets
crickets
crickets
crickets
crickets
crickets
crickets
crickets
crickets
crickets
crickets
crickets
crickets
crickets
crickets
crickets

Maurizio Nannucci

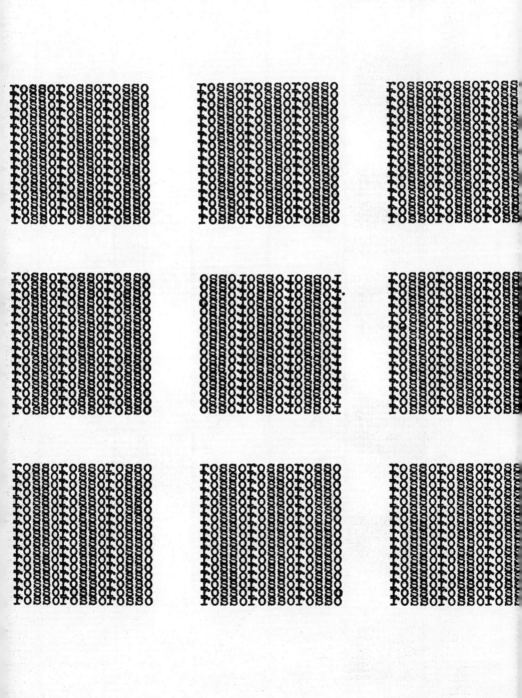

Klaus Burkhardt

LochLoch
LochLochLoch
LochLochLochLoch
LochLochwennLochL
LochLochnichtsLochLoc
chLochLochmehrLochLoc
LochLochLochdaLochLochL
ochLochLochistLochLochLo
ochLochLochLochLochLoch
ochLochLochwennLochLoch
LochLochLochumLochLochL
chLochLochnichtsLochLoch
ochLochLochwasLochLoc
hLochLochdrumLochLo
ochLochLochistLochLo
ochLochLochLoch
LochLochLoch
Loch

The Old
New

(from the book of JOB:BOJ)

Josef Hiršal—Bohumila Grögerová

(translated independently and simultaneously by Juliet McGrath)

The aesthetic of the $\frac{\text{old}}{\text{new}}$ work of art is pri-

marily determined by the $\frac{\text{subject.}}{\text{material.}}$ It has

nothing to do with creation in the $\frac{\text{old}}{\text{new}}$ sense

of the word, $\frac{\text{unlimited}}{\text{limited}}$ by the final conception of the completed work, but it is a

matter of a range of interrelated events/impulses

realizing/coordinating the predetermined goal of random process of

development, events which are realized/rhythmized development,

through the known use/natural laws of learned signs./used elements.

This process may not/may be broken off at any

time. It is not incumbent/is incumbent upon the artist to

specify/estimate the "ripenesss," "unripeness," or

"over-ripeness" of the works resulting from

a given subject./material. Beginning, labor,/rhythmization,

and end—in this way one can characterize

the role, the activity, of the old/new artist, the

result of which represents an expression of

the world picture/human condition by means of a conven-/an origi-

tional/nal form. The subject/material and the event/form

determined by it provide limited/numerous pos-

sibilities for constructive or destructive

rapprochements, for harmony or dishar-

mony, for the preordained or the accidental.

Heinz Gappmayr

DÉCIO PIGNATARI

(*adapted*)

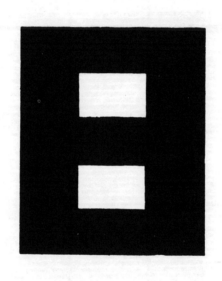

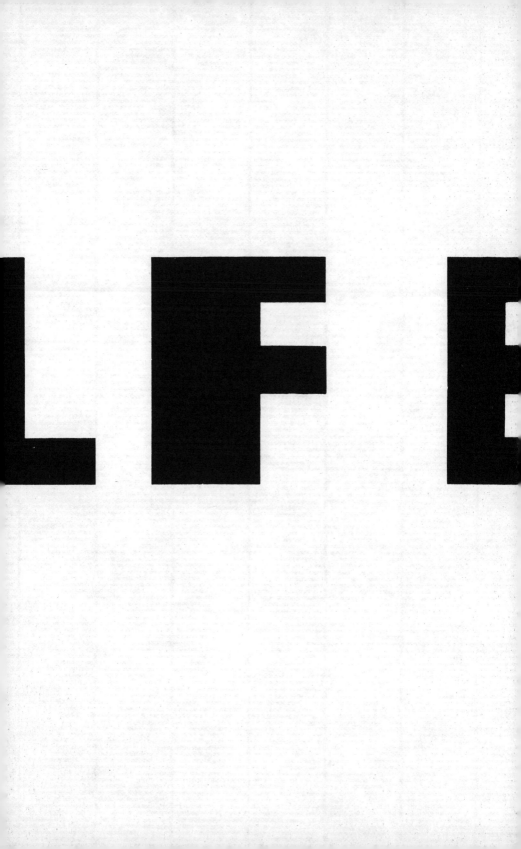

silences in tribute t
o SILENCE j cage

alain arias-misson

words & plastic struc
ture selected at rand
om

silence of Butte silence of motivity silence of Euphorbia s
ilence of ite, missa est silence of litigant silence of embl
em silence of polite silence of Portland silence of dog's e
ar silence of entwist silence of chaw silence of Gueudecour
t silence of ramsons silence silence of fermail
silence of designable silence of sacramental silence
silence of muddy silence of indecent silence of chrom
ato silence silence of over-capitalization silen
ce silence of rarefactive silence of divalent si
lence silence silence
e silence of phylo silence of prefix silence of
diplomatize silence of netherward silence of develop silen
ce silence of break silence of maik silence
silence of me
silence of indigent silence silence of nig si
et silence silence silence of obvious s
lence of Pressburg silence of Maeander silence of pub silence
ilence of flask silence silence of
silence silence
pit silence of county silence of quarter silence
silence of recur silence of superior maxillary silence of
curacy silence of medicinable silence of reservation silen
ce of Lauraceae silence of man-at-arms silence of premorse
silence of professor silence of deeply silence of Kt. sile
nce of consignable silence of ointment silence of erly sile
nce of brandish silence of choriamb

white

HEINZ GAPPMAYR

du   you

ich   I

etwas

something

(*adapted*)

e t w

door
obscurity
sound

      SEIICHI NIIKUNI

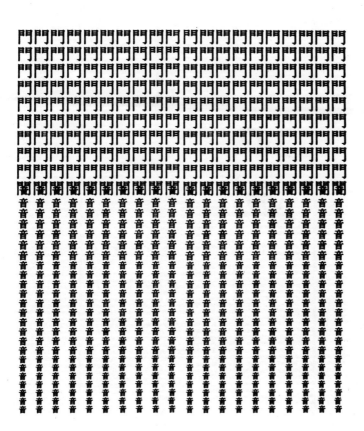

皿
血

dish
blood

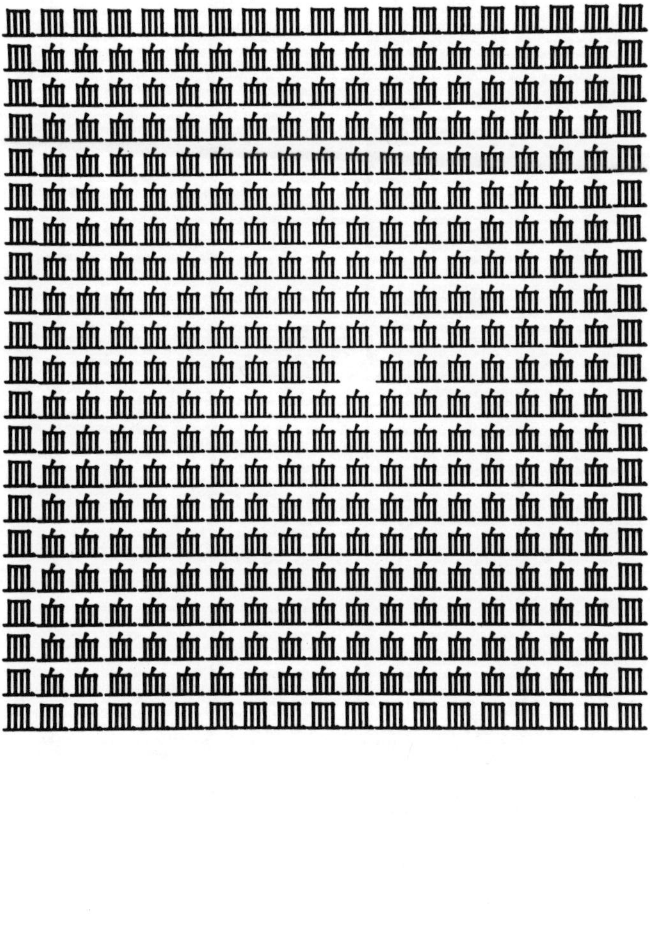

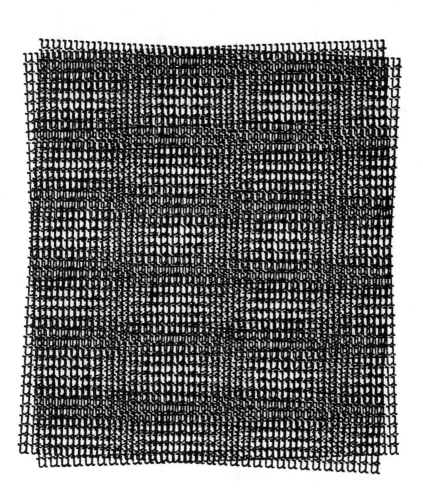

```
roseroseros          erose
roseroseroseroserose
roseroseroseroserose
roseroseroseroserose
roseroseroseroserose
roseroseroseroserose
roseroseroseroserose
roseroseroseroserose
roseroseroseroserose
roseroseroseroserose
roseroseroseroserose
              eros
```

JOHN FURNIVAL

ALL LINKS - FUTURE.

ALL LINKS PAST - BROKEN

VISIBLE INVISIBLE RANDOM FULL VISIBLE INVISIBLE

TA-TA COLD
EN FUTURE
BYE-BYE
GOLDEN
PAST

PAST MINUS FUTURE EQ

PRESENT - A PLATE

FOR I THINK THE POEMS
WILL MAKE THE POEMS
THE MOST SPIRITUAL ARE TO BE
POEMS AND SPIRITUAL WILL MAKE
AND OF MORTALITY BODY
FOR, I THINK I SHALL
THEN I SUPPLY MYSELF
WITH THE POEMS
OF MY SOUL AND OF IMMORTALITY"

BY ANSWERING A DAILY MIRROR

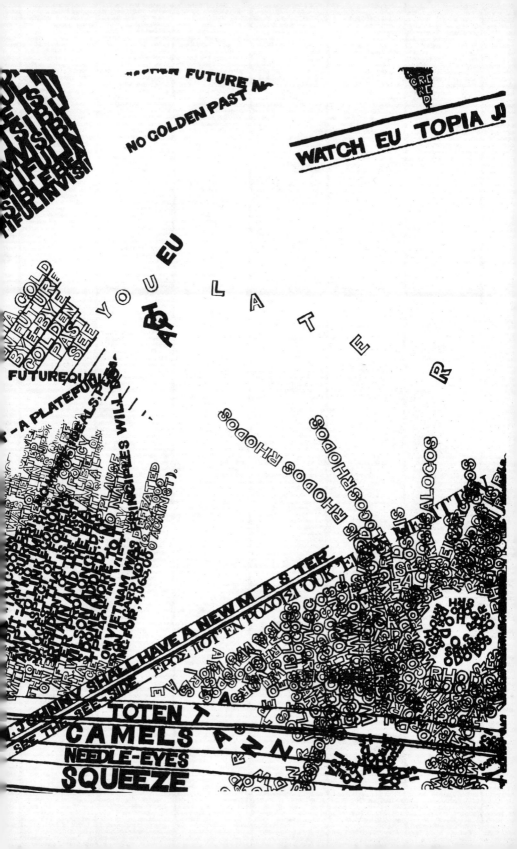

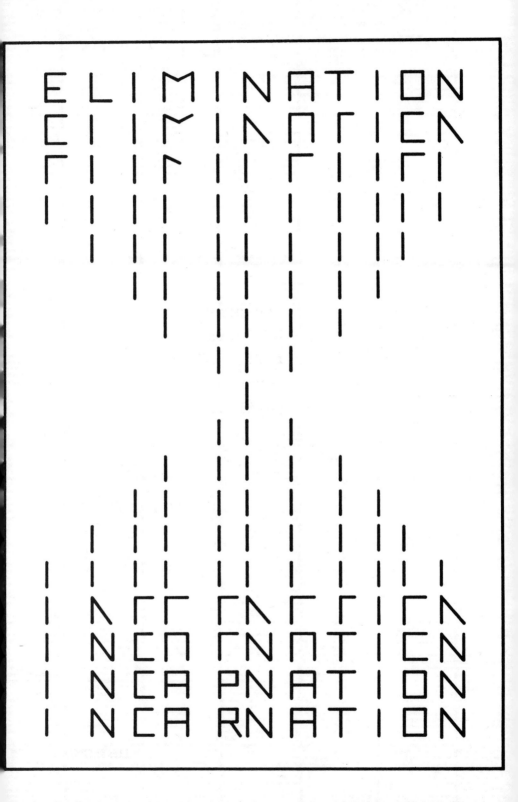

The arms
of Caesa
r from A
lexander
until...

```
bombA
bombB
bombC
bombD
bombE
bombF
bombG
bombH
bombI
bombJ
bombK
bombL
bombM
bombN
bombO
bombP
bombQ
bombR
bombS
bombT
bombU
bombV
bombW
bombX
bombX
bombY
bombZ
```

poem to be
read aloud

l as a language

Maurizio Spatola

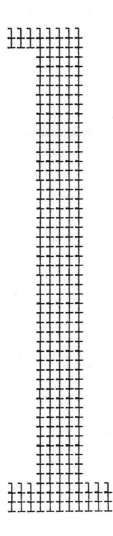

★

k

k   m

x

b

o

q   g

f

V

o a

o   ⌐n

↑

k

z

+   b   d ↑

p

k

death poem #3

Arrigo Lora-Totino

il
il
il
il
il
l'
il
il
il
il
il

ZEN

PEDRO XISTO

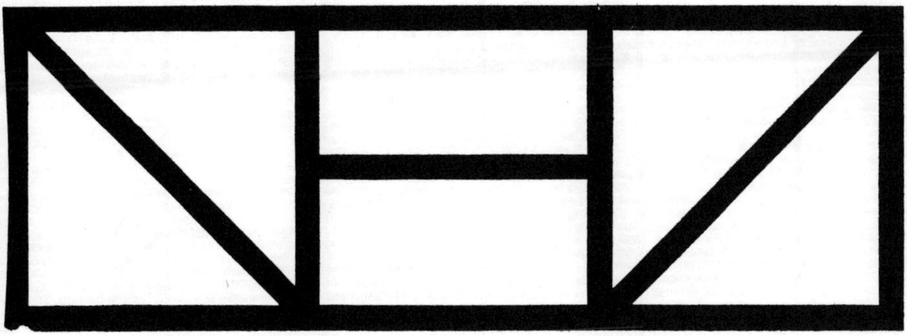

CARL FERNBACH—FLARSHEIM

mirror field inside
Random Field

water water water water water water water water water water water water
water colorless color transparent water voice and voice water sea drop
sphere a hand water vertical sky a mouth water plain river a house wate
thread rock a flower water rain face a child water clouds atmosphere gc
well echo a village water ice crystal an eskimo water sun leaves a
woman water boat silence a man water sky medusa moon water horizon
eye fish water ship water men water palm sun voices voices sun palm
water men water ship water fish eye horizon water moon medusa sky
water a man silence boat water a woman leaves sun water an eskimo
crystal ice water a village echo wall water goods atmosphere clouds wa
child face rain water a flower rock water a house river plain water
a mouth sky vertical water a hand sphere drop sea water voice and voic
distance water transparent color colorless water water water water wate

acqua acqua acqua acqua acqua acqua acqua acqua acqua acqua acqua acqua
acqua acqua acqua acqua acqua acqua acqua acqua acqua acqua acqua acqua
acqua acqua acqua acqua acqua acqua acqua acqua acqua acqua acqua acqua
acqua acqua acqua acqua acqua acqua acqua acqua acqua acqua acqua acqua
acqua acqua acqua acqua acqua acqua acqua acqua acqua acqua acqua acqua
acqua acqua acqua acqua acqua acqua acqua acqua acqua acqua acqua acqua
acqua acqua acqua acqua acqua acqua acqua acqua acqua acqua acqua acqua
acqua acqua acqua acqua acqua acqua acqua acqua acqua acqua acqua acqua
acqua acqua acqua acqua acqua acqua acqua acqua acqua acqua acqua acqua
acqua acqua acqua acqua acqua acqua acqua acqua acqua acqua acqua acqua
acqua acqua acqua acqua acqua acqua acqua acqua acqua acqua acqua acqua
acqua acqua acqua acqua acqua acqua acqua acqua acqua acqua acqua acqua
acqua acqua acqua acqua acqua acqua acqua acqua acqua acqua acqua acqua
acqua acqua acqua acqua acqua acqua acqua acqua acqua acqua acqua acqua
acqua acqua acqua acqua acqua acqua acqua acqua acqua acqua acqua acqua
acqua acqua acqua acqua acqua acqua acqua acqua acqua acqua acqua acqua
acqua acqua acqua acqua acqua acqua acqua acqua acqua acqua acqua acqua
acqua acqua acqua acqua acqua acqua acqua acqua acqua acqua acqua acqua
acqua acqua acqua acqua acqua acqua acqua acqua acqua acqua acqua acqua
acqua acqua acqua acqua acqua acqua acqua acqua acqua acqua acqua acqua
acqua acqua acqua acqua acqua acqua acqua acqua acqua acqua acqua acqua
acqua acqua acqua acqua acqua acqua acqua acqua acqua acqua acqua acqua

acqua incolore colore trasparente **acqua** percorso voce e voce **acqua** mare goccia
sfera una mano **acqua** verticale cielo una bocca **acqua** piano fiume una casa **acqua**
filo roccia un fiore **acqua** pioggia volto un bimbo **acqua** nubi atmosfera dèi **acqua**
pozzo eco un villaggio **acqua** ghiaccio cristallo un esquimese **acqua** sole foglie una
donna **acqua** barca silenzio un uomo **acqua** cielo medusa luna **acqua** orizzonte
occhio pesce **acqua** nave acqua uomini **acqua** palma sole voci **voci sole palma**
acqua **uomini acqua nave** acqua **pesce occhio orizzonte** acqua **luna medusa cielo**
acqua **un uomo silenzio barca** acqua **una donna foglie sole** acqua **un esquimese**
cristallo ghiaccio acqua **un villaggio eco pozzo** acqua **dèi atmosfera nubi** acqua **un**
bimbo volto pioggia acqua **un fiore roccia filo** acqua **una casa fiume piano** acqua
una bocca cielo verticale acqua **una mano sfera goccia mare** acqua **voce e voce**
percorso acqua **trasparente colore incolore** acqua acqua acqua acqua acqua acqua
acqua acqua acqua acqua acqua acqua acqua acqua acqua acqua acqua acqua
acqua acqua acqua acqua acqua acqua acqua acqua acqua acqua acqua acqua
acqua acqua acqua acqua acqua acqua acqua acqua acqua acqua acqua acqua
acqua acqua acqua acqua acqua acqua acqua acqua acqua acqua acqua acqua
acqua acqua acqua acqua acqua acqua acqua acqua acqua acqua acqua acqua
acqua acqua acqua acqua acqua acqua acqua acqua acqua acqua acqua acqua
acqua acqua acqua acqua acqua acqua acqua acqua acqua acqua acqua acqua
acqua acqua acqua acqua acqua acqua acqua acqua acqua acqua acqua acqua
acqua acqua acqua acqua acqua acqua acqua acqua acqua acqua acqua acqua
acqua acqua acqua acqua acqua acqua acqua acqua acqua acqua acqua acqua
acqua acqua acqua acqua acqua acqua acqua acqua acqua acqua acqua acqua
acqua acqua acqua acqua acqua acqua acqua acqua acqua acqua acqua acqua
acqua acqua acqua acqua acqua acqua acqua acqua acqua acqua acqua acqua
acqua acqua acqua acqua acqua acqua acqua acqua acqua acqua acqua acqua
acqua acqua acqua acqua acqua acqua acqua acqua acqua acqua acqua acqua
acqua acqua acqua acqua acqua acqua acqua acqua acqua acqua acqua acqua
acqua acqua acqua acqua acqua acqua acqua acqua acqua acqua acqua acqua
acqua acqua acqua acqua acqua acqua acqua acqua acqua acqua acqua acqua

ARRIGO LORA-TOTINO

TEINFINITEINFINITEINFINITEINFINITEINFINITEINFINITEINFINITEINFINITE
TEINFINITEINFINITEINFINITEINFINITEINFINITEINFINITEINFINITEINFINITE
TEINFINITEINFINITEINFINITEINFINITEINFINITEINFINITEINFINITEINFINITE
TEINFINITEINFINITEINFINITEINFINITEINFINITEINFINITEINFINITEINFINITE
TEINFINITEINFINITEINFINITEINFINITEINFINITEINFINITEINFINITEINFINITE
TEINFINITEINFINITEINFINITEINFINITEINFINITEINFINITEINFINITEINFINITE
TEINFINITEINFINITEINFINITEINFINITEINFINITEINFINITEINFINITEINFINITE
TEINFINITEINFINITEINFINITEINFINITEINFINITEINFINITEINFINITEINFINITE
TEINFINITEINFINITEINFINITEINFINITEINFINITEINFINITEINFINITEINFINITE
TEINFINITEINFINITEINFINITEINFINITEINFINITEINFINITEINFINITEINFINITE
TEINFINITEINFINITEINFINITEINFINITEINFINITEINFINITEINFINITEINFINITE
TEINFINITEINFINITEINFINITEINFINITEINFINITEINFINITEINFINITEINFINITE
TEINFINITEINFINITEINFINITEINFINITEINFINITEINFINITEINFINITEINFINITE
TEINFINITEINFINITEINFINITEINFINITEINFINITEINFINITEINFINITEINFINITE
TEINFINITEINFINITEINFINITEINFINITEINFINITEINFINITEINFINITEINFINITE
TEINFINITEINFINITEINFINITEINFINITEINFINITEINFINITEINFINITEINFINITE
TEINFINITEINFINITEINFINITEINFINITEINFINITEINFINITEINFINITEINFINITE
EINFINITEINFINITEINFINITEINFINITEINFINITEINFINITEINFINITEINFINITE
teinfiniteinfiniteinfiniteinfiniteinfiniteinfiniteinfiniteinfiniteinfiniteinfiniteinfinite
EINFINITEINFINITEINFINITEINFINITEINFINITEINFINITEINFINITEINFINITE
EINFINITEINFINITEINFINITEINFINITEINFINITEINFINITEINFINITEINFINITE
EINFINITEINFINITEINFINITEINFINITEINFINITEINFINITEINFINITEINFINITE
EINFINITEINFINITEINFINITEINFINITEINFINITEINFINITEINFINITEINFINITE
EINFINITEINFINITEINFINITEINFINITEINFINITEINFINITEINFINITEINFINITE
EINFINITEINFINITEINFINITEINFINITEINFINITEINFINITEINFINITEINFINITE
EINFINITEINFINITEINFINITEINFINITEINFINITEINFINITEINFINITEINFINITE
EINFINITEINFINITEINFINITEINFINITEINFINITEINFINITEINFINITEINFINITE
EINFINITEINFINITEINFINITEINFINITEINFINITEINFINITEINFINITEINFINITE
EINFINITEINFINITEINFINITEINFINITEINFINITEINFINITEINFINITEINFINITE
EINFINITEINFINITEINFINITEINFINITEINFINITEINFINITEINFINITEINFINITE
EINFINITEINFINITEINFINITEINFINITEINFINITEINFINITEINFINITEINFINITE
EINFINITEINFINITEINFINITEINFINITEINFINITEINFINITEINFINITEINFINITE
EINFINITEINFINITEINFINITEINFINITEINFINITEINFINITEINFINITEINFINITE
EINFINITEINFINITEINFINITEINFINITEINFINITEINFINITEINFINITEINFINITE
EINFINITEINFINITEINFINITEINFINITEINFINITEINFINITEINFINITEINFINITE
EINFINITEINFINITEINFINITEINFINITEINFINITEINFINITEINFINITEINFINITE
EINFINITEINFINITEINFINITEINFINITEINFINITEINFINITEINFINITEINFINITE
EINFINITEINFINITEINFINITEINFINITEINFINITEINFINITEINFINITEINFINITE
EINFINITEINFINITEINFINITEINFINITEINFINITEINFINITEINFINITEINFINITE

reden

schweigen um sich nicht reden zu hören

reden um

schweigen um sich nicht reden zu

reden um sich

schweigen um sich nicht reden

reden um sich nicht

schweigen um sich nicht

reden um sich nicht schweigen

schweigen um sich

reden um sich nicht schweigen zu

schweigen um

reden um sich nicht schweigen zu hören

schweigen

to keep silent in order not to hear oneself speak

to speak in order not to hear oneself keep silent

uanj
naju
njau
anju

ujan
aunj
jaun
jnau

janu
ujna
unja
unaj

uajn
aujn
ajun
ajnu

anuj
nauj
nuaj
nuja

njua
jnua
juna
juan

uuuuuuuuuuuuuuuu
uuuuuuuuuuuuuuuu
uuuuuuuuuuuuuuuu
uuuuuuuuuuuuuuuu
uuuuuuuuuduuuuuuuu
uuuuuuuuuuuuuuuu
uuuuuuuuuuuuuuuu
uuuuuuuuuuuuuuuu
uuuuuuuuuuuuuuuu

you

```
wand     wand     wand     wand
      bild     bild     bild
wand     wand     wand     wand
      bild     bild     bild
wand     wand     wand     wand
            wild     wild
               hand
                        wild
         hand     hand
            wild
                           wund
```

wall

picture

hand

animal

sore

ASTRODOME

'As real grass withers in the Astrodome (at Houston,
Texas), it has been replaced by Astrograss.'

(news item)

all is not grass that astrograss
that astrograss is not all grass
that grass is not all astrograss
astrograss is not all that grass
is that astrograss not all glass
not all astrograss is that glass
all that glass is not astrograss
that is not all astrograss glass
that glass is not all fibreglass
not all that fibreglass is glass
fibreglass is not all that glass
is that not all fibreglass glass
that fibreglass is not all grass
glass is not all that fibreglass
is all astrograss not that glass
all is not grass that fibregrass

ORIGINAL SIN AT THE WATER HOLE

asp
   on
      taneousobstreperousos
tentatiousstentorianosmos
isofhys
tericallysnortingpossesofs
portingshehippopotamusses
pottingalittlefloatin
                    g
               asp!

ARCHIVES

```
generation upon
generation upon
generation upon
generation upon
generation upon
generation upon
generation upon
generation upon
generation upon
generation upon
generation upon
generation upon
generation upon
generation upon
generation upon
generation upon
generation upon
generation upon
generation upon
g  neration upon
g  neration up n
g  nerat on up n
g  nerat  n up n
g  nerat  n  p n
g   erat  n  p n
g   era   n  p n
g   era   n    n
g   er    n    n
g    r    n    n
g         n    n
g         n
g
```

hlas
voice

JIRI VALOCH

```
h                     s                         h
  l               a      a              l
    a          l             l        a
      s a l h                 h l a s
    a          l             l        a
  l               a      a              l
h                     s                         h
  l               a      a              l
    a          l             l        a
      s a l h                 h l a s
    a          l             l        a
  l               a      a              l
h                     s                         h
  l                                       l
    a                                   a
      s a l h                 h l a s
    a                                   a
  l                                       l
h                     s                         h
  l               a      a              l
    a          l             l        a
      s a l h                 h l a s
    a          l             l        a
  l               a      a              l
h                     s                         h
  l               a      a              l
    a          l             l        a
      s a l h                 h l a s
    a          l             l        a
  l               a      a              l
h                     s                         h
```

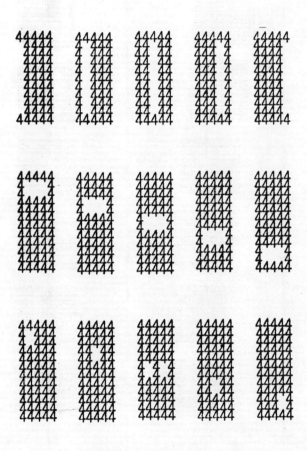

plastic poem 1
plastic poem 2

耳目口上
目口上
三日月

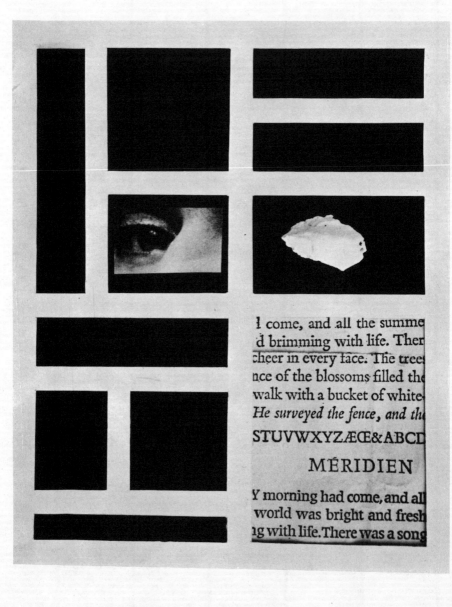

l come, and all the summe
d brimming with life. Ther
cheer in every face. The trees
nce of the blossoms filled the
walk with a bucket of white
He surveyed the fence, and th

STUVWXYZÆŒ&ABCD

MÉRIDIEN

Y morning had come, and all
world was bright and fresh
ig with life. There was a song

she loves me

she loves me not

she loves

she loves me

she

she loves

she

```
light circle          light circus
I seek light          light I seek
I seek circus         I seek circle
            light
```

CARLO BELLOLI

cerchio

luce circo

luce cerchio

luce

luce cerco

cerco luce

luce

cerco

cerchio

circo

cerco

cerco

luce

cerco

EPITHALAMIUM—II

   &=e   S=serpens
   he=êle   h=homo
   she=ela   e=eva

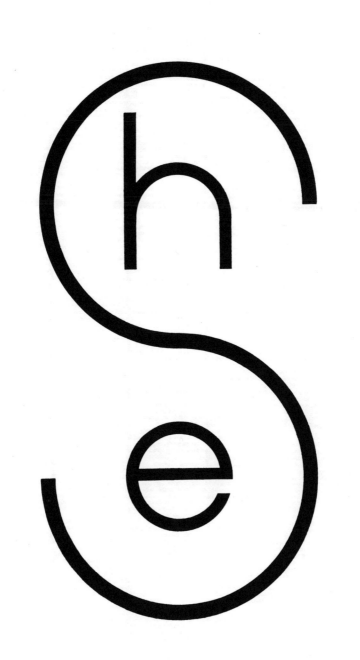

lilac

Mary Ellen Solt

The Old
New

(from the book of JOB:BOJ)

JOSEF HIRŠAL—BOHUMILA GRÖGEROVÁ

124

(translated independently and simultaneously by Elizabeth Herrmann)

The aesthetics of the old/new work of art are mainly determined by the subject matter./material. We are therefore not dealing with creation in the old/new sense of the word, meaning that it has not been/been achieved through the final conception of the finished work, but we are confronted by a sequence of interrelated processes which accomplish the precon-impulses which harmonize the free course ceived aim of education through the con-of education by giving it rhythm scious use of learned signs following the natural laws of the elements used. The process may not/may be broken off at any point. It is not/is up to the artist to determine/to guess at the maturity, the immaturity, or the overmatur-ity of the work and its subject matter./material. Be-ginning, work,/giving rhythm, and ending could well describe the role of the old/new artist. It is an occupation leading to expression of ideology/human state by means of traditional/individual form.

The subject matter / material and the corresponding process / form provide few / many possibilities for con-structive or destructive interference, thereby creating harmony or disharmony, creating that which has been premeditated or that which is coincidental.

eros

PAUL DE VREE

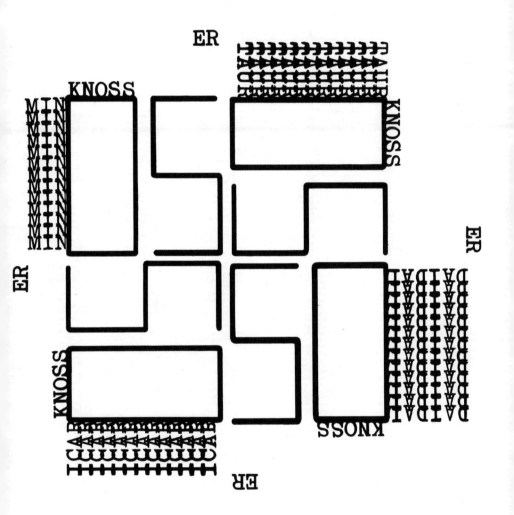

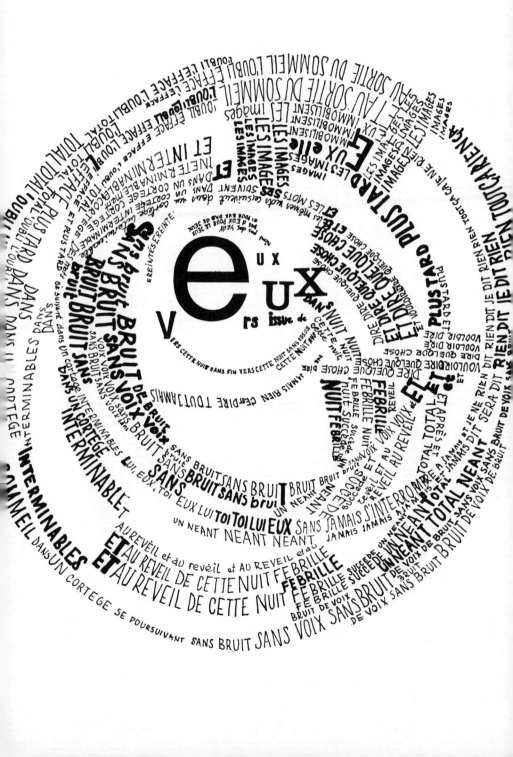

LES IMAGES
LES IMAGES
LES IMAGES
LES IMAGES

IMMOBILISENT
IMMOBILISENT
EUX IMMOBILISENT

ET

EUX elle

JOURS EFFACE EFFAC
EFFACE EFFAC

ET INTERMI
INTERMINABL

ET DANS UN CORTEGE
DANS UN CORTEGE

JARD LES IMAGES

SES MOTS
ET LES MOTS

SOIVENT
les mêmes mots les suivent deux un

ni pour eux pas de jeux
Pas des yeux
Pas d'EUX POUR LE JEUX

EREINTES EREINTE

e UX
e UX

Vers issue de
rs issue de

V ERS CETTE NUIS SANS FIN VERS CETTE NUIT SANS ISSUS

DANS NUIT NUIT CETTE NUIT
CETTE NUIT
cette nuit
CETTE NUIT

DIRE QUELQUE CHOSE
DE QUELQUE CHOSE
QUELQUE CHOSE ET
DIRE QUELQUE CHOSE

ELQUE CHOSE DIE
FEBRILE NUI
FEBRILE nuit succed
NUIT FEBR

NE

JAMAIS RIEN CE DIRE TOUT JAMAIS

DE BRUIT
VOIX BRI
Sus Br

7

oh ceisivieut deu

Pas des YEUX
PAS d EUX POUR LE JEUX
NI POUR EUX PAS DE JE

Non!

e U X T

Jaroslav Malina

Mary Ellen Solt

God's	summer
Exit	times
Resounds	summer
A capella	answers
No one	each
Interprets	seen
Umbellar	red
Measures	silence

TIMES

SILENCE SUMMER

MEASURES GOOD EXIT SUMMER

UMBELLAR RESOUNDS

RED INTERPRETS NO ONE A CAPELLA ANSWERS

SEEN EACH

JEAN FRANCOIS BORY

8 octobre

Je ne sait plus tres bien quand ça a commencé. Depuis quelques temps apparaissent des signes étrænges.

Peut-être qu'il y en avait ᴣpuis toujours et que je les vois seulement maintenant.

25 oc▨▨

Non! Je suis sûr
qu'il y a ▨ne inv
a▨▨▨ ce▨ Signe
cor▨▨pondent a
rie▨ il▨ ▨ ▨▨ ▨
▨ ▨ ▨ ▨ ▨ ▨ ▨▨ ▨
▨▨ ▨ ▨▨▨ ▨ h▨▨
▨▨▨▨ ▨▨ ▨ ▨x
▨ ▨▨▨ c▨▨▨ ▨▨
▨▨▨▨ ▨ ▨ ▨▨ ▨
▨ ▨▨▨ ▨ ▨▨▨d ▨

1ᵉʳ

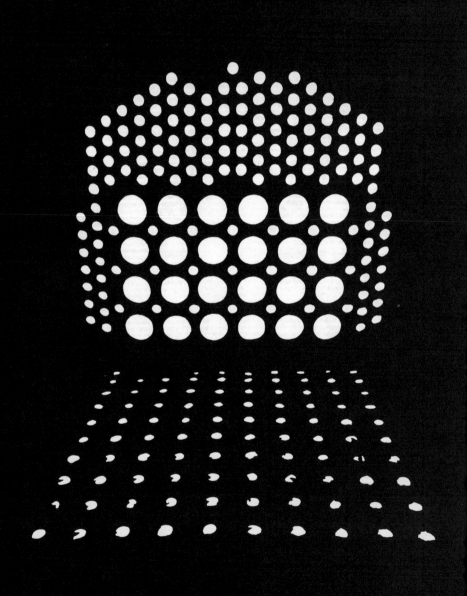

January 1968 April 1969

afterword

The heart of myth is in substance. A concrete Book necessarily is a concrete Myth.

The aim of this anthology has not been comprehensiveness, nor even (primarily) selectivity. Above all, the objective was to illustrate some of the effects that could be produced by this new kind of poetry, to put together a concrete Book.

Book is an invention that is ideally suited for narrative material; therefore the problem was to make it work also for non-narrative material. The book had to become an environment, had to be made transformable, out of its structure as a book, into a kinetic and generative art object.

We have no sense of what it is to be without books. I mean not what it is for them to be absent for us personally, but what it is for them to be absent totally, culturally, as an idea. And so in the end we do not know what it is to be with them either. We have to begin with that obvious yet astonishing fact, that we barely comprehend the nature of something we have to do with every day. It is true of our relationships with our wives and husbands; we have learned, by as little, to be civilized with our artifacts.

So the notion of a book needs defining. The concept employed here is simply this: a book is something that unfolds itself. It is always offering portions of its self, withdrawing others, suggesting still others. Emerging, present, receding: there is *how* a book is. It is a manufactured thing. It works in certain ways; it cannot work in others. It has pages. There is the embarrassingly primitive essence of it.

We do not do nearly enough with what we have invented. Our sense of event, of plot, ought to be keyed to that, to the simple fact that a book is a thing of pages, and to the fact that a page will turn.

The turning of a page is an aesthetic event; or at any rate, it should be. Anyone who writes will know how oddly crucial it can be that a certain page end with a certain word, that the next one begin with a certain other.

If we turn the page, space will become time. Now there is magic, the magic of technology. There is the key to the new poetry. Now you know how to read "etwas," or "LIFE." Science may be magical, but art is always logical. Imagine the "etwas" poem on a single page, as it was in the original. Extend the white space; transfer the black rectangle to the following page. What has happened is that we have developed a plot. We have added suspense—that is, time. Play with the space in "LIFE." Midway through the word, change the side of the page the letters can appear on. You have altered the periodicity of the poem; you have changed the velocity, the rhythm, in which the poem is immersed. And "immersed" is precisely the word, too. The poem must be grasped as expressing time. What the reader does is enter the time of the book.

What Aristotle has done for our culture has been to make us think of the artist's subject matter as being nature rather than material. If art is mimetic, plot must follow the ups and downs of the hero and heroine. But what if we keyed everything to a movement of presentation? Verisimilitude, degree of fidelity (or even degree of distortion) to physics, to psychology, to sociology, to history, would no longer be relevant to the subject of aesthetics. What would matter far more would be whether there were pages, film, canvas; light, dark; movement, stasis. At any rate, criticism would now have to begin with material as its basic value.

Literature, as it has developed so far, and this includes so-called non-realistic literature, is tied to verisimilitude in that it uses language symbolically. "Door," in any non-concrete work, stands always for something outside the word. There is little about it, as word, as visual and phonic construct, that makes it aesthetically important. It is useful as a reference to something else. Perhaps it may sound pleasing, and in a given poem the number of its syllables may make it usable or not. But ultimately the word has only referential value. It is quite unlike an ideogram ("stream," for example) in which the sign and the thing signified are equatable.

Concrete poetry aims, in general, at the ideogrammic state. The poets pattern the letters of words in much the same way that a Japanese calligrapher patterns the strokes of a character. By no means, however, are all Chinese characters pictures of the things they represent. Language is not that simple, and this is a too-popular fallacy about ideograms. In the poem "rain," the calligrapher Seiichi Niikuni became the poet Seiichi Niikuni when his design was able to *achieve* the identification between the-word-as-picture and the-word-as-sign. A Chinese character is not, by itself, a concrete poem. It requires the presence of an artist who will *do something* with the material.

Where a non-ideogrammic language is involved, the poet achieves an equivalent effect when a design is presented by means of which a word, say "rose," is put through a set of changes which enable it to convert into, say, "eros," as in the Timm Uhlrichs poem. Or, as with John Furnival, when a geometric pattern of phrases and catchphrases forms. There are no metaphysical implications; the integrity of the word as a set of visual elements in no way is violated.

Thus concretism begins where literacy begins. If we got used to literature being keyed to a movement of presentation, how much more intense an experience would be possible than anything poetry and prose now offer. Every turn of every page would be crucial. There would be, for the first time really, a non-oral tradition. For what we have had till now has been hardly more than the transferring onto paper, with not a great deal of essential difference, of what could just as easily have been the work of an oral poet.

Whereas these poems exploit the visual presence of print

Whereas these poems exploit the visual presen

Whereas these poems exploit the visual pre

Whereas these poems exploit th

Do you see what I mean? Printed poetry is not like oral poetry; it is not oral poetry set in print. Print is something by itself. The poems in this anthology depend for their effect on the special quality of the printed letter and of type spread across a page. It is profoundly literary, for it deals expressly with the effects of writing (as opposed to

163

telling). Entirely different techniques and conventions are required, for in telling it is the ear that must be appealed to. Here it is the eye that must be caught.

The peculiarities, the necessities, the possibilities of *written* forms are what the contemporary writer must be aware of. Most books which we have are only minimally literary. They eliminate, merely, the need for those formulaic helps to memory which the oral poet depends on. The *Odyssey* can be remembered by a normal person; Yugoslavian bards remember poems similar in length and complexity. *Ulysses* could be remembered only by an idiot savant. Yet we have not gone far with our literacy in the 3,000 some years we have had it; and not far even in 400 years, if we wish to go back only to Gutenberg.

This anthology has attempted always to be both concrete *and* a book. The arrangement, while it was largely a felt, intuitive, rhythmic thing, does clearly move in configurational blocks. The symbolic, that is mimetic, content is greatly reduced, and an effort is made to have each section evolving out of or advancing from a preceding one; this though the metaphor for the entire book might be the labyrinth or the checkerboard, and though a climax of sorts may be said to have been reached in the final symbolism of the flowers, the flames, and the mandala.

The University of California historian Carl Schorske wrote, in response to the original *Chicago Review* anthology, ". . . I'm a fan. Brain-worker's *Volkskunst!*" It is an exceedingly shrewd insight. There is a definite folk aspect to concretism. Concrete poetry is the poetry of how we think, a poetry that works with what is irreducible in the language that we think in.

The calendar in the office of the *Chicago Review* has remained set at July 1967, where (as if intended to recall to us the words Professor Schorske would soon be writing) a photograph of a bridge with the following legend has unceasingly offered itself.

> Un nuovo ponte sul *Biferno (Molise)*
> Un nouveau pont sur la riviere *Biferno (Molise)*
> A new bridge over the *Biferno (Molise)*
> Eine neue Brucke uber den *Biferno (Molise)*
> Un puente nuevo sobre el rio *Biferno (Molise)*

The italics are mine. But is this not a concrete poem? Is concretism not indeed a kind of folk art? It is all around us; it expresses what is truly fundamental in our lives. Anyone who feels that concretism is necessarily cerebral has only to look at the work of John Furnival, or Seiichi Niikuni, or Jaroslav Malina. There is, after all, a basic convertibility, and little there to be cerebral over, in the triple metaphors of the circle, the checkerboard, and the labyrinth.

The end of life is the mythic end of substance.

Eugene Wildman

Eugene Wildman holds degrees from Columbia University and The University of Chicago. He has been editor of the CHICAGO REVIEW, *has taught literature and creative writing at Northwestern University, and is completing an experimental novel,* THE SUBWAY SINGER/THE GARBAGE BARGE. *He is at present on the faculty of the University of Illinois, Chicago Circle Campus. Mr. Wildman is also editor of the anthology,* EXPERIMENTS IN PROSE, *published by Swallow Press.*